BARGING INTO CHELMSFORD

the Chelmer and Blackwater Navigation

John Marriage

Ian Henry Publications

First edition 1993
Second edition 1997

ISBN 0 86025 480 1

© John Marriage, 1993, 1997

Printed by
Interprint, Ltd.
Malta
for
Ian Henry Publications, Ltd.
20 Park Drive, Romford, Essex RM1 4LH

Dedicated to Anthony, Lawrence and Philip Marriage
in the hope that they will share my enjoyment of the
waterway in the years to come.

The author wishes to thank Mr Eric Boesch, Mr David Cannon, Col. John Cramphorn, Messrs. W & H Marriage, and the Essex Record Office for permission to use their photographs. Unless so indicated, the pictures are from the author's own collection.

Two motor boats passing through Springfield Lock, shortly after its restoration in 1993

PREFACE

As a child growing up on the outskirts of Chelmsford, within half a mile of the River Chelmer, one of my greatest pleasures was to see a barge travelling sedately along the river. I wondered how such a large boat was able to pass along the waterway with such ease and how it happened to be just the right size to fit into the nearby lock. Where did it come from and where it was going? It took me many years to find the answers.

In 1939 war started and the barges were not seen again until hostilities ended. As I grew up I became a frequent user of the hire rowing boats, then at Barnes Mill, and somewhat rashly took up swimming in its rather murky depths. Later, I acquired a bicycle and was able to ride on the towpath along the entire waterway from Chelmsford to Maldon, travelling through countryside which was quite unspoilt and totally rural. A few years later I acquired a canoe and discovered that I required permission to use the waterway; this brought me into contact with the Navigation Company, whose administration was conducted at an old fashioned solicitor's office in Duke Street from where, somewhat condescendingly, a licence was issued on payment of a modest fee.

Earlier this century Chelmsfordians constantly undervalued their town and it is unfortunate that its waterway, until recently at least, has suffered the same fate and its amenity, beauty and recreational potential have always been totally undervalued.

This book is the result of years of exploring and delving into the background of the canal and its associated

1

rivers as well as meeting those unforgettable waterway characters, Bill Siggers, canal foreman, who ran the canal as his own private fiefdom, and George King, lock-keeper and dredgerman, a cheery character always willing to help.

I hope its publication will raise the profile of this beautiful and historic waterway and encourage more people to appreciate and enjoy its wonderful heritage.

The first edition of this book appeared in 1993 to coincide with the passing of the bicentenary of the Chelmer Navigation Act. This expanded and rewritten edition is published to mark the 200th anniversary of the actual opening of the navigation in June 1797.

JOHN MARRIAGE

The Company seal, design inspired by the Naiad Conduit Head that was in Tindall Square. The date commemorates to first meeting of the Company

CHAPTER I

INTRODUCTION

Chelmsford, at the turn of the 18th century, was already the County Town of Essex, but was in reality just a small market town on the main road from London to Norwich. Most of its bulk imports were carried to the town by pack mule and heavy cumbersome wagons along the turnpike road from Maldon, then an important port located at the head of the long Blackwater estuary. Midway between these two towns the long, steep slope of Danbury Hill intervened. In those days the road in winter was deeply rutted and muddy and for most of the year a serious impediment to traffic. The once great forest of Essex had mostly been felled and the shortage of cheap fuel for winter fires was particularly acute. In the absence of any alternative, many of the poor were forced to burn straw to keep warm.

Nevertheless, despite the poor state of the road, by the 1770's some 10,000 tons of goods - about half being coal - - traversed the Danbury Road. Elsewhere in Britain there were plans to construct canals to enable large quantities of goods and materials to be transported cheaply and easily from place to place. Thoughts naturally turned at that point to the possibility of making the Chelmer - a small river flowing from Chelmsford to the Blackwater estuary - into a navigable waterway, so that bulk goods - particularly seaborne coal - could be brought more readily into the town.

There was talk of such a scheme as early as 1677 and Andrew Yarranton produced a plan showing how the river could be made navigable at an estimated cost of about £8,000. However, because of opposition from Maldon, the idea came to nothing. In 1733, John Hoare, a well known surveyor of the day, produced two detailed schemes. One contemplated fairly conventional improvements to the river, which he estimated would cost about £9,355. The other, a much more radical scheme, envisaged the construction of an entirely new channel along the valley which would have cost about £12,870. In those days both were huge sums and the idea was again shelved. Thirty-two years later enthusiasm had again grown and Thomas Yeoman, a consultant engineer, is reported to have said, "The utility and benefit of the navigation will first arise from the greater cheapness of carriage. For example... the price of land carriage and all goods brought by wagons from Maldon to Chelmsford is 8/- per ton. whereas tonnage and lighterage by water may be charged at only 2/- per ton. Adding to this a toll of 2/6d, the price will be 4/6d. This will be a saving of nearly half of what each individual pays for each ton of goods by road."

In 1766, as a result of his survey, an Act of Parliament was passed to make the river navigable from `the Port of Maldon to the Town of Chelmsford' for boats able to carry cargoes up to thirty tons. It was intended that the main canal wharves and warehouses would be located at Fullbridge, Maldon and at Moulsham Bridge at Chelmsford. The Act went on to specify that the river improvements should be carried out within 12 years and that no work should begin until the estimated costs of £13,000 was subscribed. Less than half was raised and

Chelmsford at the beginning of the 19th century, still a small market town astride the River Chelmer

again the scheme was abandoned.

All the enthusiasm for the various proposals came from people living in and around Chelmsford, as this was where the benefit would be felt. Fierce opposition came from Maldon people, who realised that they would lose substantial income and jobs derived from tolls, harbour dues and wharfage. Allied with them were the millers along the river, who were concerned about the potential loss of water to operate their water wheels, particularly in times of drought. A leading campaigner opposing the scheme was John Strutt, whose son had just succeeded him in Parliament as M.P. for Maldon.

However, despite these setbacks, interest in the idea continued and in 1792 a fresh scheme was prepared under the leadership of the ninth Lord Petre of Ingatestone and Thomas Branston, M.P., of Skreens, Roxwell. To overcome Maldon's opposition, the plans envisaged a new route at the downstream end bypassing the town. It was to consist of a new channel from Beeleigh, making some use of the bed of the River Blackwater, past Heybridge Mill and then proceeding down to a point below Maldon on the River Blackwater Estuary, known as Colliers' Reach. This new route had the dual advantages of staying outside the then Maldon Borough boundary and at the same time striking the estuary at the highest point that the heavily laden coal ships could penetrate without having to transfer part of their cargo over the side into lighters.

At the junction with the estuary, a large basin was to be built, with a sea lock, able to accommodate incoming ships. At the Chelmsford end, another basin was suggested on the north-east side of the town in Springfield parish rather than in Chelmsford parish as if, within the latter, it was thought there might be problems with the Mildmay entail. A short cut would connect the basin with the river below Moulsham Mill.

The costs of this, the most ambitious scheme yet produced, were estimated to be £40,000, with the right to raise a further £20,000 in the form of shares or borrowing on the tolls. A fresh Act of Parliament was received in 1793 and named about 150 `proprietors'. Some of the surnames mentioned are still to be found in the area today, even though many of the original subscribers came from Leicestershire.

It also specified that the waterway was to be navigable `for the passage of boats... barges and other vessels'. As was normal in such Acts, a public right to use the canal was included, subject, of course, to the proper payment of tolls. Their actual tollages were specified in the Act and ranged from ¼d per mile per quarter for oats, malt and other grain to 2d per chaldron (36 bushels) of coal and 2½d per mile for all other goods. Stone for road making, other than turnpikes was to be carried free and riparian owner's pleasure craft were also toll free provided the locks were not used. The Act contained powers to compulsorily purchase land. Some 70 acres of land in all were acquired in this way. Included within the Act were powers for a Justice of the Peace to impose transportation to Australia on those found guilty of damage to the Company's property. Now, this would be the reverse of a deterrent, and has not been invoked for many years! However, other clauses are still applicable. These include forbidding the obstruction of any part of the navigation by any boat or vessel. Its owner could be fined for every hour the obstruction continued. In addition, the occupier of any

CHELMSFORD. 154.

The River Can about 1900. Had the Thomas Yeoman canalization scheme been adopted these river banks would have been busy with barge traffic instead of providing moorings for a few rowing boats

mill was held to commit an offence if he permitted the water level on the pound he controlled to fall 21 inches below its impounded level. The Company was also required to provide a `fit and sufficient public wharf with a crane and other engines' next to Springfield Basin.

Although opposition to the scheme continued, Royal Assent to the Chelmer Navigation Bill was received on 17th June 1793 and still remains, without amendment, on the statute book. It authorised the `making and maintaining of a navigable communication between the town of Chelmsford or some part of the parish of Springfield to a place called Colliers' Reach...' as previously described. It is recorded that when the news reached Chelmsford cheering crowds gathered in the town and beer was distributed to the people, church bells rang and bonfires lit in the streets, whilst the more well-to-do met for a more genteel celebration in the Black Boy Inn, one of the town's largest and most important coaching inns.

CHAPTER II

THE WATERWAY IS BUILT

The first meeting of the owners of the proposed navigation - The Company of Proprietors of the Chelmer & Blackwater Navigation Ltd - was held on 15th July 1793 at the Black Boy Hotel, which was at the junction of Springfield Road and High Street, on land now occupied by Menzies bookshop.

Construction of the canal started later the same year, under the general direction of the famous engineer, John Rennie, F.R.S. (1761 - 1821) who was responsible for many other contemporary waterways, including the better known Kennet & Avon Canal, where the design of the locks, bridges and other installations is very similar. However, he is reputed to have visited the site only five times and the actual survey of the river was carried out by Charles Wedge.

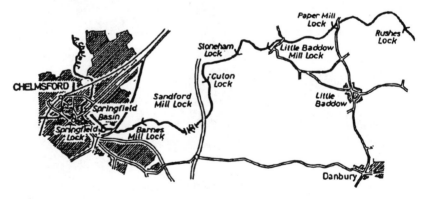

Day to day control was vested in the resident engineer, Richard Coates, who immediately prior to this project had held a similar position under Rennie constructing the Ipswich to Stowmarket Navigation, which it closely resembled. He brought some of his Suffolk navvies, including his brother, a stonemason, to carry out the work. Some of their descendants still live at Heybridge Basin, and are proud of their Suffolk origins.

The total length of the waterway is 13¾ miles. To overcome a drop of over 76 feet, 12 locks were built, plus the sea lock at Heybridge Basin, all neatly spaced about one every mile. In addition to the cuts at either end there were also a number of channels around existing mills and the whole river was widened, straightened and deepened. Wharves were built in several places to serve the nearby villages. The locks are 17 feet wide and 68 feet long and able to accommodate barges 60 feet long by 16 feet beam, each of which could carry 25 tons of cargo, although having a maximum draft of only 2 feet. The sea lock at Heybridge Basin was built to take 300 ton vessels up to 107 feet long by 26 feet wide, with a draft of up to 8 feet.

Reproduced by permission of the Inland Waterways Association

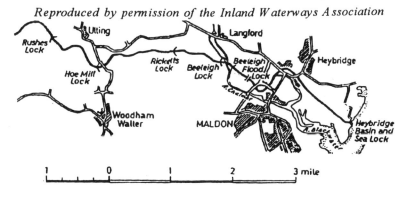

A horsedrawn lighter approaches Springfield Basin with timber for Brown & Son, c.1955

A lighter typical of those used on the Navigation from 1796 until postwar years. The stout construction, similar to that of a Thames barge, can clearly be seen. Their strength was undoubtedly why they normally remained in service for many years

The reason the dimensions of the 12 locks were chosen is uncertain, but it is possible that they were built to a size to enable lighters already in common use on the estuary to penetrate the navigation. Most of the locks, bridges and lock houses were built of bricks made at Sawpit Field, Boreham and Ulting. The locks, bridges and wharves were capped by Dundee Stone, chosen for its hard-wearing qualities and a continuous towpath was created from end to end, bridging streams and side channels as necessary. A particular feature was the self closing towpath gates, built as a smaller version of the more common farm gates. They were mounted at an angle to their posts in pairs at every field boundary and were designed to prevent cattle from straying from field to field.

On 23rd April 1796 the first brig sailed into Heybridge Basin. Its arrival was reported in the *Chelmsford Chronicle* as follows: "... there arrived in the grand basin at the entrance to the Chelmer Navigation near Collier's Reach the good brig *Fortunes Increase*, Robert Parker, master, laden with 150 chaldrons (just over 5,000 bushels) of the best Burnmore coals from Sunderland consigned to Messrs Blyth and Coates, the first adventurers on the navigation. This is the first shipload of coal which the navigation has received. It may be worthy of remark that the *Fortunes Increase* is a good old brig and during her journeys on the seas about 40 years has never experienced any misfortune. Yesterday 3 wagons loaded with coals from a coal yard at Boreham, stocked by the Chelmer Navigation arrived here [Chelmsford] with their horses decorated with coloured ribbon as being the first carted coals from that navigation. On Tuesday last [26th April 1796] a barge was loaded with nearly 150 sacks of flour at Hoe Mill from where it

NAVIGATION. PAPERMILLS.
BRIDGE.
1927

W.A.J

Although most of the bridges were built entirely of brick, several had a central span of timber similar to this, at Paper Mills. It was rebuilt in the 1930s.

proceeded by the new navigation to Colliers' Reach for the London Market." This was the first of many tons of flour to be carried on the waterway and over a period of time the mills were enlarged to take advantage of the easy communications.

The navigation was extended in stages towards Chelmsford. In September 1796, two barges loaded with foreign wheat were able to penetrate to Moulsham Mill, just downstream of the town. However, the remainder of the canal was not opened until the middle of the next year, on 2nd June 1797, the *Chelmsford Chronicle* reported that the next day barges loaded with coal would "proceed in grand procession with colours flying, etc. into the basin near Springfield Bridge, the ground around which is now divided and let to different persons for wharves, will in a few days after the opening be plentifully stored with coals, lime, chalk, cinders [coke], etc." Not unnaturally, the convoy of boats was met by enthusiastic crowds of townsfolk.

Thus opened, the new waterway and the land around was quickly laid out with sawmills, lime kilns, iron foundries, stone masonry and coal yards. Quays were constructed alongside the basin and at its head was a large open wharf and yard area. This extended almost to Springfield Road on the west side and to Navigation Road on the north. This was the public wharf, as required by the enabling Act. Adjacent to this large yard a gas works was built in 1819 (founded by Coates) becoming the first to be built on an inland site in Britain, using coal barged up the navigation. Although the original works have long since disappeared, a British Gas distribution depôt and several gasometers now mark the site.

WELLS & PERRY,

late Burnett,)

Coal & Timber Merchants,))

Stone Lime of Superior quality

CHELMSFORD BASIN,

This 19th century engraving gives an idealised view of Wells & Perry's wharf at Springfield Basin and shows some of the activities, including storage of coal and timber, and probably a small ironworks *Essex Record Office*

On completion of the waterway, Richard Coates settled in Chelmsford, eventually to live in a large house nearby in Springfield Road. He became a major carrier on the navigation. His nephew, James Brown, eventually took over the business, and with his son, carried on trading, renaming the firm, Brown & Son. They continued to use the waterway for the carriage of coal, coke, slate and timber. Other users with their own wharves included Wells and Perry, coal merchants, Wray and Fuller, stonemasons, and T. D. Ridley & Sons, also coal merchants.

A problem encountered in the navigation's construction was the existence of a half mile tidal canal leaving the River Chelmer at Beeleigh and terminating at Langford Mill on the River Blackwater. This was originally known as Mr Westcomb's Navigation because it ran through his land to the mill. The new waterway sliced through the little canal. After some initial disagreement, the lower section running into the Chelmer was banked off and the upper part incorporated as a branch of the new navigation, becoming known as Langford Cut, and, until the coming of the railways, was used extensively by Langford Mill for the import of coal and the export of flour.

Springfield Basin, c. 1910. The *Seven Brothers*, owned by Edwards Woodcraft of Heybridge Basin, is fully laden with building materials

CHAPTER III

RICHARD COATES

Richard Coates was born on 14th January 1763 at Marske, near Richmond, Yorkshire, the son of Richard and Dorothy Coates.

In 1791 he was appointed assistant engineer for the construction of the 14 mile Stowmarket to Ipswich Navigation, also known as the River Gipping Navigation, under the overall direction of John Rennie. This waterway, now derelict, has often been described as the Chelmer's twin, such is the similarity of the countryside, the constructional details of the waterway, and the barges which once plied it. It is currently the subject of restoration efforts by the local branch of the Inland Waterways Association.

Work on the Gipping Navigation was completed in 1793 and Richard Coates was appointed resident engineer to build the Chelmer & Blackwater Navigation. For this he engaged his brother George, a stonemason, who had also been employed by him in Suffolk and he brought some fifty experienced Suffolk navvies to work with them. This involved a varied programme of widening, straightening and deepening the existing river, together with the construction of bridges and locks. As on the Gipping, he used Rennie's standard designs. As resident engineer it was his job to oversee the constructional work along the entire length and this necessitated frequent inspections by horseback, using the rough roads and tracks of the time.

On the completion of the canal, Coates set up his own carrier business on the waterway, transporting a variety of cargoes to and from the county town. Not surprisingly his quay, a short section of water frontage flanking Navigation Road, next to the huge public wharf, became known as Coates Wharf.

Richard Coates settled in Chelmsford, living in a large house he had built in Springfield Road, on a site now occupied by Tesco's supermarket. He also became a successful business man in the town and at Heybridge. Amongst his most profitable enterprises was the setting up of the Chelmsford Gas Company with its gasometers and retorts next to the Public Wharf. For a time it had the monopoly in street lighting.

Coates had two daughters, Sarah, who never married, and Deborah, who married John Wyndham Holgate, another local businessman.

In 1813 he turned his attention to establishing a purpose-built National Church School at Springfield, next to the Green, becoming one of its first Governors. Later, he paid for two wings to be added. For many years it was the only school in the parish. Today, the old school building is closed: its successor is the present joint C of E/RC Bishops' School in North Springfield, where some of the memorial plaques from the old school have been transferred. He also provided funds towards various improvements at Springfield Church. He died on 12th April 1822, aged 59, and was buried in the churchyard in an impressive tomb. Members of his family were later interred with him.

The following appeared in the obituary column of the *Essex Chronicle* in April 1822: "On Friday 12th inst at

Springfield... Mr Richard Coates. 15 years actively engaged as a civil engineer and for the last 25 years was a highly respected merchant of this county. He was endowed with great energy of mind with strong native talent. which raised him to affluence. What he SAID was honest - what he DID was not less so. His private and public charity speak the benevolence of his heart; the distressed never applied to him in vain. He was the widow's and the orphan's counsellor: a sincere and cordial friend; an affectionate husband; the kindest father; a good master; a just. humane, pious and independent man."

Under the terms of the will of his surviving daughter, Sarah, who died in 1867, restoration of the church took place. The porch and a plaque dedicated to his memory remain.

The tomb of Richard Coates and his family in Springfield churchyard

CHAPTER IV

HEYDAY AND BEYOND

In its heyday, the waterway carried an immense range of materials and goods of all kinds, including stone, slate wheat and timber. In addition to the important bulk cargoes of coal, the barges carried substantial quantities of Kent chalk to be spread over the Essex clay soils to improve fertility. For a time there was a weekly carrier service from Chelmsford connecting through to London, by way of Maldon. With the benefits of cheap transport and the new means of contact with the coastal trade, the character of Chelmsford began to change from that of an agricultural market town to that of an industrial centre.

The canal also acted as a catalyst for development at Heybridge village when various firms established themselves besides the canal. The most notable was founded by William Bentall, a yeoman farmer from Goldhanger, who developed a plough of advanced design as a sideline. He moved to a site alongside the Wave Bridge and concentrated on agricultural machinery, including the famous `Goldhanger Plough'. Later, under the management of his son, E. H. Bentall, the firm expanded rapidly, making extensive use of the navigation to carry raw materials and to ship out the completed products.

Along the river, too, the mills, notably Hoe, Sandford and Moulsham, made substantial use of the navigation. They considerably enlarged their capacity and, using the navigation, were able for the first time to export their flour to London and elsewhere. They found that the loss of water for their wheels was less damaging than they had earlier feared, and, like many other water mills elsewhere, they installed steam engines to drive them instead. Steam was found to be more efficient and reliable than the somewhat erratic water supply, Coal to heat the boilers was brought by barge from Heybridge Basin.

At the turn of the 19th century, the waterway was very busy and some consideration was given to extending it to Dunmow, making use of the River Chelmer most of the way, with another branch leading towards Ongar. Undoubtedly for much of the way the then existing water levels maintained for the benefit of the various mills would have been utilised, with locks inserted at each level change. The second branch would probably have made use of the River Can and have passed close to Writtle. Sadly, nothing came of these ideas, which would now have been of immense recreational value.

In 1843 the Eastern Counties Railway was built from London through Chelmsford to Colchester and Ipswich and, as in so many other cases, its coming brought a slow decline in the use of the canal. Competition between the two modes of transport was keen but there is recorded one instance of co-operation at Maldon, where a special railway siding was built so that sea coal and other goods intended for Witham and Braintree could be off-loaded from barges into the railway trucks belonging to the Braintree and Maldon Railway, which thereby acted as a branch for the canal in supplying raw material to both Braintree and Witham. Later the same railway wharf was used to float materials down to Bentall's factory at Heybridge village. Ironically, its best years of trading

A maintenance barge carries a new lockgate downstream from Paper Mill Lock, c.1920   *Essex Record Office*
An empty steel barge at Paper Mill Lock, c.1965   *David Cannon*

occurred whilst Eastern Counties Railway was being built, as the waterway was used to ship in large quantities of materials used in its construction. Another recorded use was the transportation, on 29th September 1819, of heavy artillery pieces and other ordnance from Chelmsford when the Napoleonic garrison was withdrawn. The guns - intended to defend London from an advancing French Army were removed from their emplacements at Galleywood Common and Widford, and together with other military stores, taken to the public wharf next to Navigation Road and loaded onto barges and transhipped to sailing brigs at Heybridge Basin and so onwards round the coast to Woolwich Arsenal.

Coal continued to be imported to Chelmsford by water until 1927, much of it for use at the gasworks, but eventually this trade transferred to rail, with grossly overloaded drays bringing it from the railway goods yard in New Street. Brown & Son Ltd, which had developed into a large general builders' merchants, continued to bring all its imported foreign timber - mostly Finnish and Russian - up the navigation until 1972, but when, the firm was taken over this practice was discontinued and the small fleet of lighters disposed of.

As traffic began to decline the Navigation Company looked to other means to supplement its income. Towards the end of the last century cricket bat willow trees were planted along its entire length and land and properties along the navigation were disposed of. This included most of the large public wharf at Springfield until only a small area on the east side of Wharf Road at the head of the basin remained. Finally, in a move of dubious legality this last area was incorporated into the adjoining timber yard

Heybridge Basin in the early 1950s, showing timber awaiting shipment to Chelmsford

and the crane removed, leaving no wharfage or facilities for casual users.

The normal travelling time from Heybridge Basin to Springfield Basin was about 12 hours - a long tiring day for the two-man crew. They took turns leading the horse and steering, so there was chance for a rest. In the early days there was an overnight stop at Paper Mill Lock. There were 'bothys' or bunkhouses for the men and stabling for the horses. The Gaswork's crews used one on the south bank with Brown's crews one on the north. Brown's former bunkhouse is now the Company headquarters, whilst the other is now a store. Eventually this system was discontinued and it became usual for the Heybridge men to bring a loaded barge to Paper Mill and exchange it for an empty one from Chelmsford. In this way both crews could return to base every evening.

Originally brigs and other sailing ships entered Heybridge Basin to unload directly into the barges, but this stopped early this century as the newer coastal steamers were too large to enter the sea lock. Instead, timber, by then the sole import, was transferred from the coasters to a string of old dismasted Thames Barges near Osea Island and towed into the Basin. The timber was then laboriously reloaded on the canal lighters. In the 1960's the lock was lengthened to 130 feet and timber laden motor vessels were then able to enter the Basin so that once again there could be a direct transfer of timber into the lighters. At the same time all the horse drawn lighters - unchanged since the navigation opened - were scrapped and replaced by new all-steel barges, powered by huge Harlow-built *Harbourmaster* outboard diesel engines. They travelled rather faster and were each capable of carrying a cargo of

The 1955 Directors' Inspection. *Chelmsford Duke* led by Fred Hoy

Victoria was craned into Heybridge Basin in 1975 and was a change of direction for the Navigation Company. Standing on the foredeck to mark the occasion are (l to r) Eddy Webb, Amenity Manager, Col. John Cramphorn and the Company Secretary, Francis Stunt

some 45 tons and they continued to carry timber upstream to Chelmsford for a further ten years.

In 1948 the majority of British canals and navigations were nationalised and the custom of the various owners to formally inspect their waterways by boat was discontinued. Only on the Chelmer - which escaped nationalisation by an accident - does this practise survive. The more prestigious companies kept a special launch for such purposes, but the Chelmer Board of Directors merely borrowed an ordinary working horse-boat sheeted over for the day and fitted with tables and chairs. Now, the Company's own charter vessel *Victoria* is pressed into service. The original reason for the inspection was to enable the Board to examine at first hand the canal and its installations so that they could decide what repairs or improvements were necessary. Today the event is more of a social occasion, when the Directors entertain local dignitaries. On the Chelmer's now long disused twin, the River Gipping Navigation, it is reputed that crowds would gather and cheer the boat on its way, so important was the occasion thought to be. However, on the Chelmer things have always happened quietly, without fuss or drama, with the trip habitually taking place each year on the first Saturday in July, attracting little attention. Charter work must have priority and it is now held midweek. According to tradition the day of the inspection has ALWAYS turned out to be a warm and sunny day. Erased from memories are the less pleasant days including a particularly bad day when the event was postponed due to heavy floods.

CHAPTER V

THE WATERWAY TODAY

In 1973, following the ending of commercial traffic, the Inland Waterways Association held a promotional Rally of Boats at Chelmsford, thereby setting the scene for the opening of the waterway for pleasure craft. This event, held in King's Head Meadow, was very popular and was attended by thousands of Chelmsfordians, the majority of whom had never previously realised that the town possessed a navigable waterway. Star of the event was undoubtedly the Navigation Company's maintenance boat *Susan*, temporarily converted to passenger duty, and for the first time substantial numbers of the public were able to enjoy short trips along the River Chelmer. The Navigation Company later opened the waterway to recreational craft and took the daring step of purchasing their own charter vessel *Victoria*.

Since then recreation on the canal has steadily increased and there are now well over 100 private motor craft of various types cruising the canal, based at moorings at Sandford, Paper Mill and Rushes Locks. In addition, there are substantial numbers of seagoing boats moored at Heybridge Basin, some of which occasionally venture up the canal. Canoeists, who prior to 1973 were the only pleasure craft to be allowed on the waterway, have also gradually increased in numbers. Now, *Victoria* is regularly hired by various groups and parties and can frequently be found cruising the lower reaches of the navigation. In

Restoration of Springfield Lock, 1993

Canoeists along the Chelmer

addition, a hire company, Blackwater Boats, offers short break holidays on their small fleet of narrow boats.

The waterway is very popular with anglers, most of whom belong to the Chelmsford Angling Association and many fine catches are regularly recorded. It is particularly noted for its large beam. The old towpath, has become a public right of way and is now much used by ramblers and walkers. It provides a unique opportunity of walking from busy Mid Essex to the Blackwater estuary without crossing a major road.

However, despite all these varied activities, the canal is the reverse of crowded, retaining its 18th century appearance and has an air of fragile remoteness which is somewhat surprising considering its proximity to bustling London. Despite the number of boats and canoes officially licensed to use the waterway, moving craft are a rare sight except during an occasional boat rally or canoe race.

The Company's practice of growing cricket bat willows along the banks and on any odd patch of land they own adds beauty and interest to the whole of the Chelmer valley, as well as providing a habitat for wildlife. They are planted primarily for commercial purposes and harvested every 10 to 15 years. Much of the wood is eventually shipped to Pakistan and made into cricket bats, but during the time it takes to mature, the growing timber gives the canal something of the character of a leafy French tree-lined waterway.

The locks made by Richard Coates remain in use, although the chambers have all been repaired and even rebuilt in a few cases. All their gates have been replaced several times but are still hand-built to the original pattern. In this they have fared better than the waterside structures.

At Chelmsford few of the original wharfside buildings now remain, even though the quays are still in existence. The most substantial survivors are the Two Brewers public house in Springfield Road, once a bargemen's beerhouse, and Kenmore House (previously known as The Eaves), originally built as a warehouse next to the public wharf area and later converted into a house. Several minor buildings still exist at the end of Wharf Road. Downstream, some of the watermills still stand, although none is now used for its original purpose. They include Barnes Mill and Moulsham Mill. At Sandford, although the mill buildings were demolished in the 1930's, a substantial structure stands on their site. It was once the town's water-works and is now an industrial museum. The former mill at Paper Mills was burnt down in 1905; its site is now known as Treasure Island, from where the London Borough of Newham Education Department run canoeing courses. The mills at Little Baddow and Ulting also burnt down many years ago, though the houses in each case escaped the flames and are still occupied. Currently there are plans to redevelop the mill site at Little Baddow as a public house: this could become a useful port of call for boaters.

Further down and beyond Rushes Lock, Ulting Church stands on the waterside, remote from the village. This little 13th century parish church, restored in 1873, is noted for its fine timber roof. However, by far the most impressive canalside building, with the remains of its own wharf, is that of Bentall's warehouse next to Wave Bridge at Heybridge and parallel to the canal. After being derelict for many years it has been tastefully restored. At Heybridge Basin there is a row of clapboard houses facing

The Victorian rear extension at Moulsham Mill was built primarily to house its steam roller mills. Coal to heat the boilers was supplied via the wharf

W & H Marriage

the sea lock and the Old Ship public house. On the opposite side of the canal is the Basin Lock house and two cottages. The only other original lock cottage remaining is at Ulting. Two others at Sandford and Paper Mill have been rebuilt since 1950. Elsewhere along the Navigation a number of the original attractive brick arched bridges designed by John Rennie remain. They include Bundock's Bridge at Springfield and Chapman's Bridge at Beeleigh. The latter has the distinction of being constructed from Suffolk bricks, presumably some left over from Coates' Ipswich to Stowmarket Navigation project. Elsewhere the bricks used were all locally made.

The terminal cut to Springfield Basin joins the River Chelmer just below Springfield Lock. Full navigation upstream along the River Chelmer and its tributary the River Can is barred by a massive sluice, built in the 1960's as part of a flood prevention scheme for central Chelmsford. This sluice keeps the upstream water level remarkably stable even during times of peak flow, protecting the town centre from flooding and incidentally making conditions ideal for canoeing at all times of the year, icy conditions precluded. A boat roller path has been provided around this obstruction so that light craft can get upstream along the River Can through the Town Centre, Central Park and even up to Admiral's Park. On the Chelmer, there is less scope, but paddlers can certainly penetrate to the new University Campus, via several portages, although as one proceeds upstream the river becomes smaller and correspondingly shallower. All these waters are extensively used by members of Chelmsford Canoe Club and various affiliated groups for training for national and international events or just simple cruising. Despite its continuing semi-isolation from the canal, this stretch of water, including its tributary, the River Can, is believed by many people to have acquired a formal right of navigation, due to long usage. Certainly there are many 19th century photographs in existence showing the public enjoying themselves in rowing boats on the water next to Central Park.

A suggestion originally put forward in the early 1970's by the local branch of the Inland Waterways Association was for a new navigable channel to be created between Springfield Cut and the River Chelmer. This would have the affect of allowing a greater range of craft to penetrate right into the Town Centre and extend full navigation for a further mile or so, thereby adding to the recreational potential of the river. After many setbacks this idea was eventually enthusiastically adopted by the Chelmsford Borough Council in their various redevelopment plans for the locality. If carried out this will greatly enhance the amenity value of the entire waterway. In particular it would become possible to board *Victoria*, or any other charter boat which might be commissioned in the future, in Central Park, and go right down the canal to Maldon. Such a trip would be immensely popular. Sadly however, a number of existing bridges on the Can are rather low and may ultimately need to be raised. Happily, current Council policy is to ensure that all new bridges on this stretch of the Can and Chelmer are constructed to provide a headroom for boats of 2.3 metres - slightly higher than on the canal itself. It was unfortunate that, despite a large number of objections, a low bridge was allowed to be built in 1992 as part of a major new shopping precinct just upstream of the weir. It is now generally accepted that the developers made a mistake, not spotted at the time by the

Brown's timber wharves at Springfield Basin, c.1955. The lighters were unloaded under cover, the wood going straight into the warehouses

Eric Boesch

planners. Nevertheless the jacking up of this bridge and several older lightweight footbridges would not pose an insurmountable problem.

With the termination of barge traffic in 1972, Springfield Basin, Lock and Cut all fell into disuse. The lock itself was vandalised and became unusable. More recently the successor firm to Brown & Son has demolished the quayside timber sheds. For a time there seemed a real danger that the entire basin would be infilled. However, to mark the bicentenary of the passing of the Chelmer Navigation Act, the Chelmsford Branch of the Inland Waterways Association decided that as their contribution to the celebration, they would fully restore Springfield Basin, its approach channel and Springfield Lock. Over some 18 months unpaid helpers restored the facilities in time for this part of the navigation to be re-opened in June 1993. During 1992 the Basin and approach cut were completely dredged by the National Rivers Authority, now the Environmental Agency. Also dredged and cleared - for possibly the first time since the canal was opened - was the all important feeder channel which supplies the Basin with water from the River Chelmer. Symbolically, the first craft into the Basin was *Victoria.* Among the passengers was the Mayor of Chelmsford and other civic dignitaries. At the same time a large trail boat rally, with many craft visiting the waterway for the first time, was held. The authorities, in a parallel move, have now officially recognised the heritage value of this fragment of 18th century England and declared the entire canal, from Chelmsford to Heybridge Basin and its valley, a linear Conservation Area, one of the first in the country.

There is now a feeling of confidence that the Chelmer

Clearance of the canal feeder at Springfield Basin, 1992

and Blackwater Navigation will play an increasing rôle as a substantial environmental and recreational amenity in Mid Essex, whilst retaining its conservation role as a habitat for animals and plants. This feeling was boosted in 1996 by proposals made by Essex County Council, with Chelmsford Borough Council, to create a Millennium Centre based around Springfield Basin which they have provisionally entitled `Chelmer Waterside'. It comprises land currently derelict or put to temporary uses and formerly occupied by a large gas works. National Lottery funds are being sought to finance the scheme. The re-development is intended to be a landmark cultural focus for all Essex and will include such diverse proposals as a new Heritage Centre, a Concert Hall, Museum and Art Centre, as well as various commercial leisure activities. As an integral part of the overall scheme it is suggested that there should be a complete rehabilitation of the Basin, together with the creation of the long-hoped-for connecting channel between the canal and the Chelmer, together with a new river basin (a new but welcome idea) immediately above the existing King's Head Meadow Sluices, to create moorings additional to those proposed in Springfield Basin. Work on the first phase is scheduled for 1997. Completion date is intended by A.D. 2000.

Should these proposals come to fruition, the whole area will reach an importance undreamt of by the original promoters of the Chelmer Navigation Act and the pioneering work of Richard Coates and his long-gone navvies will certainly have contributed to the welfare of future generations of Chelmsfordians and the people of Mid Essex.

CHAPTER VI

BOATS ON THE CANAL

VICTORIA

Following the demise of commercial traffic in the early 1970's, the Navigation Company decided to commission a pleasure barge for the waterway. *Victoria* was built by Bingley Marine, in Yorkshire and delivered to Heybridge Basin in 1975. She is 58 feet long, 12 feet 6 inches wide, and draws 2 foot 9 inches when loaded. She has an unladen weight of 30 tons and is licensed to carry a maximum of 48 passengers and a crew of 4. Propulsion is provided by a BMC 2.521 diesel engine. Apart from a small open observation deck the boat is entirely enclosed and equipped with comfortable seats, together with a bar and toilets. She has now been in regular use for over 20 years, during which time she has traversed the waterway many times, mostly on charter work, for which purpose she is extremely popular during the summer months. A variety of functions take place on board, from wedding receptions and birthday parties to business conventions and school outings. *Victoria* is based at the Company's operational headquarters at Paper Mill Lock, Little Baddow.

Susan, the last of the traditionally built lighters, moored below Barnes Lock in 1992

BARGES

Horse drawn barges were once a common sight on the navigation with cargoes to and from Chelmsford. Trade began to fall away once the railway was built through Chelmsford and gradually the barges disappeared, mainly to be dumped in side creeks and backwaters around Heybridge Basin.

The Chelmer & Blackwater Navigation is a very conventional waterway, with its locks, bridges and other installations making use of John Rennie's standard design. Nevertheless, the dimensions of the locks are unusual and unlike almost any other inland navigation. The lighters, too, were totally different to the normal inland waterways pattern and it is possible that the design pre-dates the canal and is probably mediæval.

Although the barges operated by several different owners, they were all of a similar design being 60 feet long by 16 feet wide. They were completely open, with a flat bottom, a pointed bow and transom stern and of carvel construction and with similar carpentry details to the many Thames barges which used to ply the Blackwater and the East Coast.

Susan, an experimental boat, was made by Prior's of Burnham in 1953, for Brown & Son of Chelmsford for the timber trade. She was built to the same lines as the horse-drawn lighters but powered by an in-board twin cylinder Thorneycroft diesel engine, with the propeller set in a tunnel within the hull. Otherwise, the sole departure from the traditional design is the installation of a twin rudder. In 1955 Brown & Son decided to move away from horse power and re-equip with motorised boats. *Susan* was not

Bill Siggers (centre) and George King (2nd left) with other canal employees doing maintenance work at Beeleigh in the late 1930s

entirely successful due to weed problems in the propeller tunnel and later boats were all fitted with *Harbourmaster* outboard engines. *Susan* is slightly smaller than the old horse-drawn boats, being only 55 feet long and 13 feet wide. She is made of oak and pine, with elm bottom boards.

Although the Navigation Company later acquired, and still retains, a steel lighter called *Julie*, *Susan* represents the very last of the traditional design of barges on the waterway and indeed elsewhere. She is therefore an important maritime heritage item, particularly when in full working order.

When several all steel motorised barges were commissioned, *Susan* was presented to the Navigation Company for use as a maintenance boat, continuing in this rôle until 1972 when *Julie* became available to the Company. On becoming redundant, she was acquired by the Inland Waterways Association for preservation. However, they transferred her to the specially formed Chelmer Lighter Preservation Society, but she was later taken over by the Passmore Edwards Museum of Stratford, E.15, who at the time had the ambition to establish a small fleet of traditional Essex working boats. Subsequently the old boat was transferred to the Chelmsford Museum Service, who are now the owners.

Chelmsford Museum Service maintain *Susan* as a living exhibit; she is crewed by the members of the Chelmer Lighter Preservation Society and can sometimes be seen cruising the upper reaches of the canal. Her current base is the Industrial Museum at Sandford Mill.

Two Blackwater boats pass through Little Baddow Lock

BLACKWATER BOATS

This small family owned company has been operating on the canal for the past five years with 4 four-berth narrow boats called *Ruddy Duck, Goosander, Widgeon* and *Little Stint*, which are available throughout the year for short break holidays and longer periods for self drive hire on the waterway. The boats are comfortably fitted out with one double and two single berths, with separate kitchen area, shower and WC. Propulsion is by a Yanmar diesel engine with single lever control. The Company is based at Sandford Lock, about 2 miles from Chelmsford. Despite the comparative shortness of the navigation, many hirers report that they have insufficient time to cruise the entire waterway, such is its peace and tranquillity which encourages them to linger.

OTHER CRAFT

A variety of private craft are to be found on the waterway. In addition to the four hire craft mentioned above, a number of narrow boats have made their appearance in the last few years, including one which, at almost 60 feet long, is the nearest to full length that the waterway can ever hope to accommodate. Two Edwardian steam driven boats have been introduced within the last few years and their numbers are likely to increase, an advantage being not only their novelty but also their operational quietness. However, the ultimate `green' propulsion - electrically propelled craft - have yet to arrive. No doubt some will be eventually introduced and at that stage recharging points will need to be provided.

CHAPTER VII

CANOE CLUB AND THE SEA CADETS

The headquarters of the Chelmsford Canoe Club and Sea Cadets is on the banks of the River Chelmer immediately opposite the Island Car Park and next to Highbridge Road. As the only water-based organisations in the town they provide many recreational boating activities. They are also a colourful source of interest to shoppers and passers-by and so enhance the town centre. The Council provided both groups with long leases to their premises over 25 years ago to enable them to establish themselves and both have developed strongly. Indeed, the Canoe Club is now one of the best known clubs in the country and has the distinction of providing Olympic paddlers for Britain in every Games since the war, including 1996, as well as participating in many other national and international events. Much of the Club success is due to its superb location on the River Chelmer next to The Meadows on the only stretch of water for miles around which is both wide and straight, perfect conditions for training young paddlers under supervision. Similarly it is ideal for canoe slalom, another branch of the sport in which the Club is becoming increasingly proficient. A further advantage is that the water is maintained at a constant level by the automatic weir. Being southward facing and with a pleasant grassed area it provides a sheltered ambience of considerable value to trainees and is ideal for supervising novices.

The 180th anniversary of the canal's opening was celebrated with a cavalcade of boats. The Chelmsford Carnival Queen was piped ashore by members of the Chelmsford Sea Cadet Corps at King's Head Meadow, June 1977

Both groups have had plans for some years to expand and vastly improve their respective premises so as to widen their activities. Indeed, the Canoe Club already has planning permission for a substantially enlarged Club House, designed to enhance the character and appearance of the enveloping Conservation Area. Sadly, until recently they were unable to proceed to raise funds due to uncertainty about their lease. However, they have recently received assurances that renewal would be sympathetically considered. A new boathouse and enclosing fence will be constructed shortly as a result of a Sports Council Grant, whilst plans are being formulated for an entirely new mega-sized Club House which will, for the first time, include PE and wet changing facilities, plus other necessary amenities.

Should the Chelmer Waterside proposal come to fruition, including the construction of the connection between Springfield Cut and the river, the scope for first class canoeing will be further increased. The Canoe Club is fortunate in having substantial numbers of people prepared to organise and instruct and with the plans for the new premises already outlined can look forward with enthusiasm to the future.

CHAPTER VIII

FRIENDS OF THE CHELMER AND BLACKWATER NAVIGATION

Following exploratory meetings earlier in the year, the Friends of the Chelmer and Blackwater Navigation was launched on 26th September 1996 at a meeting at Moulsham Mill, when about a hundred people attended, including the Mayor and Deputy Mayor of Chelmsford. The meeting was presided over by Lord Petre of Writtle Park, who had earlier agreed to become the new Society's first President, a position thought to particularly appropriate as one of his forebears had been a strong supporter of the 18th century proposals to build the navigation.

The objects of the Friends are to bring together persons who are interested in protecting, preserving and enhancing the navigation as a navigable waterway as well as maintaining its unique 18th century character in accordance with its status as a lineal conservation area. They provide opportunities for the study of the navigation, preserve and restore items of canal equipment, and facilities for social activities and organise commemorative and other events. It is also intended to provide practical and financial help to the Navigation Company in maintaining the waterway.

The Society organises a vigorous annual programme of events for members and friends, including the ever popular cruises along the navigation in *Victoria*, as well as exhibitions and towpath walks. It maintains cordial relations with other organisations with similar interests, in

To commemorate the bicentenary the Secretary of the Chelmer &
Blackwater Navigation Company, Mr Bill Spall, and his wife went on
a period cruise in *Victoria*

particular, of course, the Chelmsford Branch of the Inland Waterways Association.

INLAND WATERWAYS ASSOCIATION

The Inland Waterways Association was founded in 1946 by Robert Aickman, a well-known writer of detective and mystery fiction, with several other waterway enthusiasts. They were concerned at the growing neglect of Britain's canals and inland waterways as commercial traffic transferred to road and rail. With foresight far in advance of the prevailing opinions of the day, they could see that the 2,000 mile network was capable of providing a substantial recreational, conservation and tourist rôle. These views were, however, not shared by the government of the day, who sort only to infill and, if possible, close the canals. Public support for the new body grew quickly and attracted a wide membership from people from all walks of life and it became a powerful campaigning body supported by most boating organisations.

It soon became clear that the Association would best operate through a series of regional branches and in the 50's the London and South-East Branch was formed to promote interest within that area. Among their activities was a rally of boats held at a different location within the south-east each year. Representatives for each waterway within the branch area were elected to the management committee and I became the Chelmer representative. In that capacity I was able to organise for members several local cruises using a borrowed horse-drawn barge.

In 1971 the Branch was informed that Brown & Son Ltd of Chelmsford were to cease using the canal for the carriage of timber from Heybridge Basin. Instead, the coasters were to unload at Colchester and the timber would be carried by road to Chelmsford. At the time there was no other traffic using the waterway and it soon became apparent that unless pleasure traffic was positively encouraged to use the waterway it would rapidly become derelict.

The Branch decided therefore to hold their 1973 rally at Chelmsford. For this purpose a local committee was formed and Maurice Frost, who had a motor cruiser on the Lee, was elected Chairman. As a youngster he had been a member of the Barnes Mill Sea Scout Troop and had a good local knowledge of the waterway.

The Rally was held over the Whitsun Bank Holiday and was a great success, with thousands of people visiting the rally site. Afterwards, the Chelmsford Committee, reconstituting as a branch of the Association, decided to remain in existence in order to maintain the newly established public interest in the navigation. They quickly found that *Susan*, the navigation company's maintenance boat was to become redundant and so they acquired her for preservation. However, acquisition was not a success as the Branch had temporarily ceased active campaigning and had become virtually a social group. After a period, ownership of the barge was transferred to the specially formed Chelmer Lighter Preservation Society. Nevertheless, the Chelmsford Branch had already conceived the idea that Springfield Basin should be developed for moorings with a new channel through to the River Chelmer. They further suggested that the upper reaches of the Rivers Chelmer and Can should be improved for boating and canoeing. With a return to more active campaigning, these ideas were more

The National Rivers Authority dredging Springfield Cut, 1992

further developed some years later by members of the Branch with the publication of their booklet *Springfield Basin and Beyond*. However, it was not until some twenty years after the original promotional rally that the Chelmsford Branch was able to initiate and organise voluntary work on the restoration of Springfield Lock and Cut, leading to its re-opening in 1993.

When originally constituted as a Branch its area also included the River Stour and the River Gipping, two former river navigations, and a particularly close relationship grew up between the Branch and the River Stour Trust, with Chelmsfordians taking part in river clearance at Stratford St. Mary and elsewhere. Sadly, these ties were broken when IWA headquarters in London decided that the Stour and Gipping should become part of a branch based at Ipswich. In recent years further changes have taken place and the Branch area now covers east Hertfordshire, with the focus of interest there being the River Lee Navigation and the River Stort Navigation, both under the control of British Waterways. Naturally, much of the Branch energy and interest is now directed towards these well-used and popular waterways.

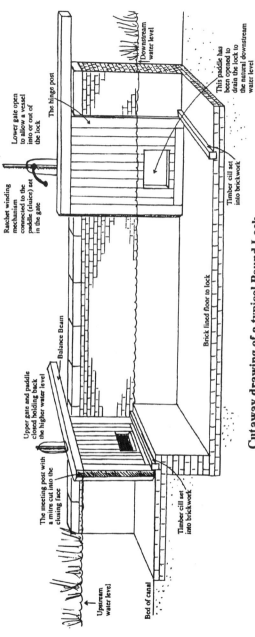

Cutaway drawing of a typical Pound Lock.

Ratchet winding mechanism connected to the paddle (sluice) set in the gate

The hinge post

Lower gate open to allow a vessel into or out of the lock

Downstream water level

This paddle has been opened to drain the lock to the natural downstream water level

Timber cill set into brickwork

Brick lined floor to lock

Balance Beam

Upper gate and paddle closed holding back the higher water level

The meeting post with a mitre cut into the closing face

Timber cill set into brickwork

Upstream water level

Bed of canal

APPENDIX

To operate or have any form of boat on the navigation, the consent of the CHELMER & BLACKWATER NAVIGATION COMPANY LTD., is required. Moorings, if appropriate, also need to be arranged. The Company can be contacted at Paper Mill Lock, North Hill, Little Baddow, Chelmsford, Essex CM3 4TQ. Telephone 01245 222025. Enquiries about chartering their vessel *Victoria* should be made to the same address.

OTHER USEFUL ADDRESSES

BLACKWATER BOATS. Bumble Bee Cottage, Boxted Road, Colchester, Essex CO4 5HF. Tel: 01206 853282.

CHELMER LIGHTER PRESERVATION SOCIETY. Hon Sec: Mr John Marriage, Budds Farmhouse, Highwood, Chelmsford, Essex CM1 3RA. Tel: 01277 352166.

CHELMSFORD CANOE CLUB. Headquarters, King's Head Meadow, Wharf Road, Chelmsford, Essex CM2 6LT. Hon Secretary: Mrs Joan Suttle, 35 Heath Drive, Chelmsford, Essex CM2 9HB. Tel: 01245 256613.

CHELMSFORD SEA CADET CORPS. Headquarters, King's Head Meadow, Wharf Road, Chelmsford, Essex CM2 6LT. Tel: 01245 261151 Commanding Officer: Lt. Dave Lincoln RNR, 2 Stourton Road, Witham, Essex CM8 2EZ. Tel. 01376 516793.

FRIENDS OF THE CHELMER & BLACKWATER NAVIGATION. Joint Hon. Secretaries: Mr W. Marriage & Mr D. Courtman, 16 Roots Lane, Wickham Bishops, Essex CM8 3LS. Tel: 01621 892231.

INLAND WATERWAYS ASSOCIATION, 114 Regent's Park Road, London NW1 8UQ. Tel Nos: 0171 586 2556 & 0171 586 2510.

INLAND WATERWAYS ASSOCIATION, CHELMSFORD BRANCH. Hon. Sec: Mr. Dave Moore, 12 Rectory Road, Stanford le Hope, Essex SS17 ODL. Tel: 01375 677729.

BIBLIOGRAPHY

Boyes, John, *and* Russell, Ronald: The Canals of Eastern England, 1977.

Camme, Peter: History of the Chelmer and Blackwater Navigation Canal

Chelmer & Blackwater Navigation Act, 1793

Cramphorn, Col J. F., *and* Cramphorn, A. M. St J.: The Story of the Chelmer & Blackwater Navigation through 200 years, 1993

Edwards, L. A.: Inland Waterways of Great Britain and Ireland

Marriage, John E.: The Chelmer and Blackwater Navigation

Matthams, John: Chelmsford and Springfield Bits

Shadrack, Alan: Schooling in Springfield - the first 100 years

Timber on its way to Chelmsford, 1950. The wood was transferred by hand from dismasted Thames barges floated into Heybridge Basin and manhandled on to Chelmer lighters *Eric Boaesch*